STYLING SAGACIOUSNESS

Before you start to read this book, take this moment to think about making a donation to punctum books, an independent non-profit press,

@ https://punctumbooks.com/support/

If you're reading the e-book, you can click on the image below to go directly to our donations site. Any amount, no matter the size, is appreciated and will help us to keep our ship of fools afloat. Contributions from dedicated readers will also help us to keep our commons open and to cultivate new work that can't find a welcoming port elsewhere. Our adventure is not possible without your support.

Vive la Open Access.

Fig. 1. Detail from Hieronymus Bosch, *Ship of Fools* (1490–1500)

First published in 2022 by punctum books, Earth, Milky Way.
https://punctumbooks.com

ISBN-13: 978-1-68571-066-8 (print)
ISBN-13: 978-1-68571-067-5 (ePDF)

DOI: 10.53288/0387.1.00

LCCN: 2022944964
Library of Congress Cataloging Data is available from the Library of Congress

Book design: Vincent W.J. van Gerven Oei
Cover image: Joseph Nechvatal, *penelOpe in agOny* (2014), 44 × 66 in., computer-robotic-assisted acrylic on velour canvas. Courtesy of Galerie Richard Paris.

punctumbooks
spontaneous acts of scholarly combustion

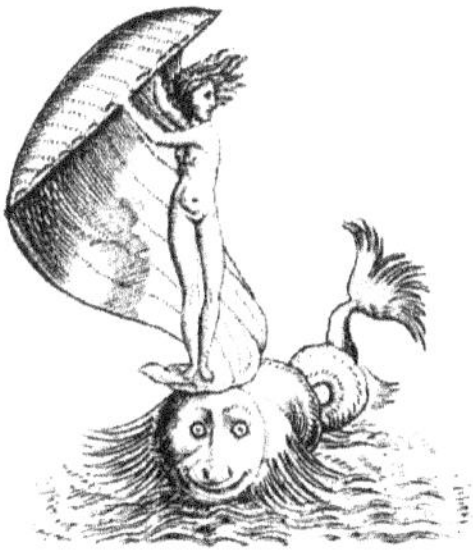

HIC SVNT MONSTRA

Styling Sagaciousness

Oh Great No!

Joseph Nechvatal

Contents

Acknowledgments

Just as *Destroyer of Naivetés* was finished on May 22, 2013 and presented as a gift to my wife Marie-Claude for her birthday that day, *Styling Sagaciousness* was finished on May 22, 2020 and again so presented. I acknowledge and thank Marie-Claude Nechvatal for her lively and stylish love. I dedicate *Styling Sagaciousness* to her.

Introduction

> There is no deal to be made with death.
>
> —Jean Baudrillard, *Pataphysics*

During the Paris pandemic confinement period of 2020, the dread of viral death was in the air. Confined to the indoors, I took the hint and finished in May my second (and, I think, last) book of *drôle* poetry called *Styling Sagaciousness: Oh Great No!* Drollness being essential to a good life, I fashioned *Styling Sagaciousness* as a death farce epic poem divided into seven major sections. For me, its Arcadian *bon délire* cheekiness possesses a silliness that constitutes precisely its lethal seriousness.

Styling Sagaciousness turned my sex farce epic poem book D*estroyer of Naivetés,* released in 2015 by punctum books, on its head and blackened it with negated scopophilia. My intention is that with these two pseudo-philosophical poetry books I will have addressed Eros and Thanatos and their connection sufficiently, and, after having extensively explored these themes in the palimpsest promiscuity of my visual art, give them a rest. If that is possible.

Ideally, my two punctum poetry books should be regarded as a pair, and read beginning with the 2015 book *Destroyer of Naivetés.* The mythopoeic mélange of *Styling Sagaciousness: Oh Great No!* is intended as a complicated forensic fairy-tale, suitable for Nô theater, which keeps slipping in and out of idiosyncratic narration. That ghostly appearance–disappearance act turns on the nub of our narcissism concerning our death; that strange, incurable and deeply irrational affliction we all share. Putting identity aside, it tests the limits of form and stretches the bounds of meaning by recasting our experiences of encountering our self as the sumptuous physicality of total negation. As such, *Styling Sagaciousness* delivers to us all an airy irrational punch of needed nonsensical negation by tying together insouciant informality with a visceral camp irony: at turns hip and flamboyant and morally outrageous. That way *Styling Sagaciousness* provides us the chance to do the counter-fearful thing, to look at our fear of negation so that such an effort might release us from fear's irrational grip, so we will enjoy ephemeral life all the more. At least for the fleeting moment. But also there is in *Styling Sagaciousness* an awareness of the impertinent splendor of the tranquility of death and decomposition, which makes it seem faintly heroic in face of death's inexorability and putrid ignobility.

So, *Styling Sagaciousness* is a meditation on humiliating death in all its undifferentiated fabulousness, by which I mean its cruel comedy. Still, *Styling Sagaciousness* is a young person's text (I am merely 71) about laughing. I hope wry humor and eccentric style is what gives *Styling Sagaciousness* a sense of dignity which asserts life's essential primacy over death. Because death is truly beyond narration and words.

Paris
2022

I

Momentous Memento Mori
One-Eyed Mystifying Mannerisms

Memento Mori Surrounded by Non-Binary Swift Nudes

life passing through ye
like wind

ye of louche tumid eyes
so jauntily festooned

now no dumb dark lust
no drip drop drip

no nice white wine
nor wax
nor blue-veined marbled walls

nor extravagant fruits
nor overgenerous flower pots

no bursting edges
no flowery sashes

no artfully loving pacifists
once so very hot

no self-restraining
undertaker

moving
from buzz kill
to rot

Memento Mori Maneuvering in the Valley of Lacedaemonian Death

no *passé* intricate outlines

no pompous pompadours

no sexual magical
painted gold doors

nor voluptuous memorials

no frothing libidos
ravenous

nor beautiful monster

no epicene genitals
in hand

no dance
no music
no pipes no pan

no throngs of satyrs
nor nymphs
scarcely born

of no no-nonsense
no heroes
ye
are shorn

no pelting
of garlands
of roses

no limpid
poses
no ornamental waters
that cry

no
honey rubbed naked shepherdesses
nor shepherds
wildly rutting

no upper lips curling
no ancillary fission

no destruction of *naivetés*

II

Satiring the Satyr

Magical Memento Mori as Thunder

no delightful dream face
nor eyes green-blue sweeping

no camp weeping satyrs
or satire
nightly peeping

no queer puffy burlesque
or
blue-rimmed ardent broth

rimming mounds and folds
no joy beholds

nor pompadour prancing
couch to couch

like young lambs
in the fresh green spring

no tinkling excitement
no flattering enlightenment

no waxing fast and furiously
with hand in pouch

Moody Memento Mori of Metamorphosis

no ravishing and stretching
no rumpling and crushing

no nuzzling wildly in soft warm crevices

no color
and no complicated blurriness
as the moon demounted into

disarray
disarray
disarray

no hair falling into jumble

no soft
delicious
swollen
nervous
responsive
impassioned
yeses

nor effeminate stallions
more

no gallant kiss rostrums
or three-headed
bitch to mend

no kitty boot licking
nor heart clock ticking

just thinking about it saddens ye
no end

Memento Mori Marches into Mêlée

no exhausted lover beside me
no platitudes mocking

no fishnet
no fish
no hysteria
really

none even calculated

no melodramatic gloom mixing
with the comic rage

no reconciliations
under the aegis
of the erotic

no drudgery
no eye hooks
no spinning
or grinning

no dynamic load blows
followed by an
effulgent collection
of go goes

no mad carnivals of frenzied intensity

no delirious vernaculars
of idiotic thoughts
even

nothing beclouded
nothing bedspread

nothing mesmeric

nothing myopic

no shivering petard
of course

none bleached
nor liquidated

no ravishing
chandelier moments
no rosy reluctances

no organs reverberating
with chaotic ardor

no confirmation of warm cummings
of
disappearing ardor

queer with a lurid preposterous *bouillabaisse* of insinuation
and effrontery

Memento Mori Mania

no excess
no erotica
no gesticulations

no chromatic progression decorated in *obbligato*

no lures
no European tours

no mesmeric black enthusiasms
or burs

nothing begins to snicker with delight

no comic vehicles of self-transcendence

nothing mesmeric
or pathetic

no recitations of sex mantras

no rainbow bodies
no hardwood bodies
no vigorous throng
chant perched at the circumference

all
vision black
no detail desired
nothing but the non-null

Memento Mori of Contestation and Decomposition

no corresponding dimensions in the imaginary
no transformations

no waves of electronic energy
no immaterial signals

no imaginative territory
lost
to infinite navigation
tossed

no peppy playmates
repeating love of ye
ad infinitum

nothing mesmeric
nothing descriptive
nothing explanative
sauced with spicy comment

so strong
this
no to fertile
that

so ominous
this inhuman
rat

no fairy beauties
no fairy eyes

no gnome desires
nor restless thighs

no duplicating egg
no sperm
no head

no stupid stubborn stains in the bed

no unconscious switch

to the passive witch

no emergent, mesmeric
moods to itch

no breastfed revitalization
dive
into wild and uncontrollable
jive

no live bodies
no intelligent minds

no dirty focus
on big behinds

no consumption
no recollection
grinds

none to be had
ye
wondrous
lubricious
priapic

Memento Mori in the Mood for Adonis Thorns

no engorged erotic eyeballs
to costume
no predetermined
zones

no interments
no psychic attainments
to own

no extensions of the bone

oh no!

no billionth rejoinder
to non-understanding

no cleansing the doors of perception
hanging

indeed
no purification
banging

no bowed overtness
deep in
do do

no expressiveness

no malicious delight

that gives the rich the right
to tonality

there is nothing left running on by itself

no dreamy usage
no baroque performance

for god's sake no mesmeric eyes

no creation of the unforeseen
once so very fancy-free

seemingly
automatically
running on
and on
and on

and on

as aesthete
stylishly, poetically, outrageously

Shambolic Memento Mori as Lazarus Rising

no spontaneously inventive vision
even no annihilation

no time
no space
no castration

no aesthete allegory
no maiden
no frustration

no departure
from mythological
exaltation

nothing frigid and forbidden
containing the quest
of instantly crossed frontiers
of swans

no strange skin
symbolic replacements
nor lubricous
daydreams
hence for ye

no open eye
no third eye
no nothing eye
no eye ball

no circle sex
no circle jerk
no horizontal points
of work

nothing analogous to cluster sex
no love shafts
or love chats
no cats

oh no
oh no
oh
oh
no
voluptuary

no plethora of possibilities
of dark eyed
sex
machine
creating
pure repetitions
mesmeric beating

no hollowing heart
out from the void

no accumulated movement
no nipple toyed
with
like a young boy

no roses
no ravishments
no great quivering bottoms

that tempt

no throng snapping
no manifold thwacking

no warm champagne douche
popping

Calamitous Memento Mori of Sundry Conundrums

no *fêtes gallantes*
merveilleuses

no world
of high culture
or bawdy imagination

no influence of the high
swirling phantasmagoricly
as time goes by

no delirium
metaphoric
pie in the sky

pulsing
higher and higher
faster and faster
none of that slapping

no ruffled disposition
or hounding
or hating

no whittled down attention
to get good ratings

just

a thousand heads of eternity

turned
towards
a sea of
décadence
raffinée

Memento Mori Moving Along the Moonlight Mile

no tiny bird cage
no whirl-pool sucker

no magnificence
no glistening
no grandeur
no foppish other

no sea of glitter
efflorescence of wickedness
eyes masquerading

no macramé humility
nor André Le Nôtre arrogance
hewn of tears

no stench of sentimentality
masquerading
as magnificence
passionately and naively
glistening
of indelible puissance

no sea
of glitter
of indelible puissance

Ruinous Memento Mori Motivating Mourning

for ye
of bitter
tassels

no gnarly grand
if no gnarly grand
gold
if no gold
slow down
if no slow down
toad
if no toad
lick
for the hell of it

no cavalcade of riders on the storm
or in the storm
yearning for aesthetic and moral spoliation

no tight holds
on ye who would nudge and wink and jostle aside

no ancient golden roll
no gorgeous bewiggings
to unfold

no marquis
of light opera sneeze
oh and
even
no Nô theater
to tease

so no heavily painted eyelids
no inexorable oddballls
that sing of

escape
from dank
triste potency

ye of burgundy
velvet
upholstered
fantasy

Memento Mori, Before All Things, From First to Last, Unalterably a Paramour of Each and Every One

no voluptuous attentions
no mock severity

no flagellations
nor orders
given

no blushes
no jealous excitations
no amorous *fessée*
taken

nothing as marvelous like wine
dancing circuitously
on the grass divine

no frills that conceal
the swell of the bough

just twinkling negation
of thorax and pelvis
turned to affirmation

of nothingness

no new moon
precise and delicate

no pale afternoon
sky
no faraway
darkness

no enigmatic dirty door
where we say goodbye

no secret wine cellar
no gardens, fella

ye of no enthralling eyes
the size of pies

no warm
windless
scented buys
of liqueur
to please
a rise

nor aromatic
pleasure
or reveries
licking ye between the thighs

no more lacking scatological
decadent
measures
rolled in tar and coated in feathers

no deeper and deeper
alleys of fleshy
weather

no rosy light
for couples in love

no nosegays
that drop
from high
up above

no sweet danger
peeping
voyeur

no fission of delicious
pleasure
oh ye
master masturbator

are ye distressed
by now?

for no more undressed attractiveness
no more
clasping together
and
mutually penetrating
oh wow

Misplaced Memento Mori in the Storm of Signs

no swelling exaltation
no unconquerable eyes
intoxicating one another
high as sky

no spot of red flesh
from which tears flow
nor happy nosegays
as far as ye know

III

Secret Love
Impish Dimness

Snowflake Tears of Memento Mori Fall on Tumbleweed

no imp
no snake
so graceful in their astonishing secrets

no self-drama
access
boundlessly
coating

thus no honey coated
kisses
floating

in an air of no boundaries

no ambrosia
or impish
odors
of hair

nor languor
nor verisimilitude
tormenting ye
oh so
sexually bare

no notion or supposition
bundled to an end

and thrown in several direction
only to bend and bend
and bend

over the ass of some grand diva queen
with little love notes
up on the screen

and unconcealed blossoms
and boobs that float
on the surface of the sea
of hope

Memento Mori's Mystic Sorrow

pandemic pansexual

no hyper spaced
secret kisses
darling

no burning desires
that smell like moist kittens

no burning eyes sparkling
no inflaming attouchements
aching

no *rêverie*
for ye

no passage of time
no dense body
divulgence

oh
that this too
sullied flesh
would melt

no sexual wisdom
burning of hair
hobby

no unlocking
the kingdom
rubbed raw
and bare

no religious terror
no sexual fury
no goddess of error
inherently

all pubic hair
is
curly

no previous history
no romantic meanings

no consciousness of guilt
or heavy breathing

no fingering around
that pit of vague burning

no unrestricted withdrawal
the closing of yearning

Memento Mori Among Buoyant Buried Bones

no circular periphery
infinitely attenuated

ophthalmic
and
adipose
entry waiting

no epicene sexual snails
of intellectual depth

no overstepping
the threshold
of critical flesh

no ancient arcane
ogles
burning nameless
as unnamed

as fraudulent
as predictable
as psychic
sexual pain

erudition is
hypothetical
wind swept away
the hills

no bare breast beaches
to be swept
no mounting
that there
awesome peak

no high romantic ills
are there
not even ones
that reek of hair

no cork screw screwing
with proclivity

and flair

no effulgent yellow
or crimson
or blue-white
whispers in the air

no buzzing cerebral balls
of myrrh
and
pansy
there

no primrose path
with verdant
dandy

no violet feeling
of subliminal hotness
handy

no blood
no juice

no life
or fashion

no pleasure prophylactic
no pastoral
purification

no bonfires
nor humble abodes
to give sexual satisfaction
along the long road

no burning of candles
that glimmer
in fat flames
or
orbs

no gold, no crimson, no orange
no nice nymphs dancing

no white sun floors
for casual romancing

no gay hibiscus
no mustard, no nettle

no onus, no peppers
no debts to be settled

no cherry
hypotheticals
no flowers
so fiery

no nihilistic death and sex
merged merrily

by all means
don't look back in ye diary

Mad Memento Mori of the Undercurrent

no horns inflamed

the sparks gone out

no feeling for fornication
or sexy pouts

no firmness
no daring
sung only as torment

ye sing no more of brooks
of blossoms
of birds
of balling

nor of inflamed sea nymphs
sprouted
and rolled

no drowsiness
no kitty
no streams
and no rivers

no spring
and no wells
no intuitional
shivers

no Eros
or Psyche

proclivities
plundered

no wide wombs
no breeding
no fertility
or thunder

no lotus
no moss
rushed down
to the sea

no louche pools
of lilies
nor liquid lowness
be

no coral snakes
and billow birds
for ye

no spirits inflamed
buzzing
like a bee

no creature
eyes
with dandy
thighs

flesh
lengthened
with fission
or schism
to hide

dear bride

Morose Memento Mori as Buoyant Blood

no blood
no discrimination
to be confronted
or aired

no curtain flame
in silence
with chasms
there

no caves
nor caverns
gasping
and grasping

no pretentious grove
to play shimmy
the basking

with unused stones

tan Lacedaemonian

of youth
of milky
inflamed
obelisks

no baroque rich man
of sack
and seed
of chaff

no transformation
the old switcheroo
dangerous in action

when nothing else will do

ever the no to nowhere
within
and without
ye
now so thin

the void
in ye
too immoderate
to see

the endless duration
too wide a spread

no one
to bed

no sprocket turning
no phallocratic yearning
with which to throw shade
on all the learning

no joy
aghast
again
and again

again and again
no physical
and mental
couplings
that last

no
do something now
else
all the light is going out

don't pout

primed
and not primed
delicious satyriasis
behind

off in a corner
no leeway
no climax
no panic
divine

no inflamed agony
or
wantonness
for wine

entreating Myrrhina to coition

so relax

no expectation
of loving
submission
love pouring

out

vast waterfall
vast ornate
carpet
roaring

no thinking ornate thoughts
with golden ornate snouts

no curvaceous
path
to flamboyant tarts

no flamboyant
epicene genitals
in hand

ye epicene ram

Mean Memento Mori of the Wicked Thicket

no lustrous pinkies cunx
no cyclic
in
and
out

no breathing
ye stop breathing
enjoy the silence

no breathing
no pulse
no wetness

no flamboyant hand
richly devoid of pus

no luxuriated yawnings
of satiated pleasure

no lavish hunks
drunk
with epicene genitals in hand

no loosened sails
no siestas
even
nor sand

nothing even like it

no unrestrained woman rams
nor unrestrained corral
hands

hot breath
no breathing
no epicene genitals
seething

no heel and strain
the gathering of the ballast

no shining path extended
without any
malice

or chalice of non-periodic scratch marks
with
no egg
as center

no dividing space
or indistinct sprout
so ye don't beg

it all was only
a taste

so
surrender
to yield
to abdicate
and steal

for
no
ravishing
no
trembling

say no to the pleading

no plunging
down deep

no nexus
no sleep

no flower in the butt
nor shimmering rows of peas

no lines of sort
that ye might snort
as long
and far
as ye can see

the sea

no south
no branch
aligned
for sure

no tongues to wag
and
demeanor

no vertical dillies
or horizontal
willies
ye dilettante of sillies

shimmering
shimmering

no boas
no
perpendiculars
not even one
want

no kissers divided
no hands in the pot

no flowers
where genitals
moan
soft and hot

so long
to all that

gliding
glistening
like pillars
of shinny
bongs

that smell greasy
like may poles
and old leather thongs

shimmering

Mystic Memento Mori in the Briar Patch

consequences
there are none

so ye sing of weird groves and unbelted bonanzas

of serpentine flowers
persisting in glances

no flowers flailing
no fragile mind milking

no wind whipped foliage
among the tall trees
tilting

from no imbroglio
produced by fathomless movement

no flowering genitals
nor dolphin eggs
gooing

no walking extenuated rainbows
delicious in their doing

no epicene copulas
no lust
no sign

of
the
long lost
lady ram

no cathartic
expenditures
of rainbows
once planned

IV

Nothing Effulgent Darling

Anti-Oedipal Memento Mori as Buoyant and Brave

no glistening current
of debauched energy
ye

no smiling in non-accordance
with thoughts
of
purgatory

nothing paired
or unpaired
like a key

with those that came before
vis-à-vis

superlative ye
no glisteningly
no fee

irremediably
evermore

no cathartic expenditure
no kaleidoscopic
imp
who slips out the bottle
makes out with the pimp

no limp
dawdling
no twirling
no probing the finger

no embouchements then
no nonchalance
noodling
the incubus
who may as well linger

nothing to abdicate
the glistening
of
a burnished trigger

no deep desire
mingling
with shallow
remorse

hungry for an antidote
of psychic
discourse

no bone and no flesh
to reenact
the once sad

sad
sex scene
ye never did have

Muddled Memento Mori as Succubus

truly no sensitive preparation
for when the hate dulled

no psychic recovery
even when the genitals lulled

no tissue of love kisses
nor caresses
nor spooning

nor harmony in desire
nor sprouting of the bean

or spooling
of the goosing epicene

as if there were no floor to it

no harmony in desire
no sprouting of the scene

no feverish disquisition
of sensibility
and sentiment

no contingent
eternal
as fragile as the continent

or as fine lilacs
with psychic composites

no aesthetic values
or unaesthetic riots

no bird to nest
singing
kiss bound
honeysuckled

no gallant *cortège*
dragging their knuckles

ye must have seemed
tremulous and expectant then
with tasseled beams
and
codpiece
when

all goes
go flutter
go flutter
into the gutter

for there is no more sounds of *frêle* sucking
no cobwebbed valley
to praise
and uncover

no drowsiness
and affection
for
ye afternoon
of fucking

no secret *rendezvous*
now
where lips are
pecking

The Panic of Mad Memento Mori and the Aftermath

no more ephemeral fluttering
bodies
Prussian blue

no fluttering
cool hands
in perfectly
assured
rhythm

overlaid
with trills
and
appoggiaturas

now

no tender lakes
of twilight
to touch ye

no beautiful
unfinished things
like scraps
of poetry

be

nor ye plucked rosebuds
that love the fiery mud

to see

no tender panopticons
gee

no non no none
on quivering knee

to tend to ye pleasure
the exquisite quiverish me

oh surely
ye jest
no ocular sea?

no
no stalks of fresh
asparagus
down below the tree

no tips of yellowed watery
silk

no suave
active fingers
milk

ye now be pensive
and resigned
to dirt
to dirt
to dirt

Mountainous Memento Mori in Spartan Oscillation

no airy scallops
nor shells
suspended over
head

no ties
of affection
quiver in the bed

ye sing of joy
no more

no hanging distractions
no endless yearnings

no great pink *mêlée*
burning

no wax candle
waxing
or waiting
nor whispers baiting

nor whimpers
whimpering
or hearts
beating

no enamored
murmurs
nor spirits
perturbed

no charming nymphs
quivering at the wee door
heard

nor red embroidered
passages
so
plush
and
oiled

nothing like that can ever get
soiled

no frolics
nor romps

nor *bagatelles*
or
folasteries

no *roués*
or *rouées*

no *accoutrements*
so carefully boiled

no foaming
and billowing
brooding of brows

no dimpled *derrières*
no problem
anyhow

no palming and persuading
so fanciful
and free

with
cut
short
hair

dramatic
accessory

éclat

no one
where one
was not required

no low humming
of the gilded bees
to absorb the juice
upon the leaves

no light operetta
joys
with boys
make noise

no vital steps forward
no striving the peak

ye might even say
ye once was
rather
poised

no uttered moist
naughtiness
nor immersive moist
sauciness

no sounds
of cooing
old glory
for free

no hopes
of
limitless love
for ye

Memento Mori as Snowflake Flâneur

no smacking lips
under the bright blue sky
of happy hips

no golden red
mortifying
blanket
rips

no goat men
lightheartedly
bending
over ye

to reinstate the tumbling rain

no sapphire sea
of soft silk nights
no timidity of part
nor pain

tiptoeing quietly into the night

no blue sphere
lighting up
between ye cheeks

no red thread
of blissful light
that leaks

out from the endless blanket sheets

from under which
ye peeks

no dive from head to hole
no lighting up the street

of the open throat

no thread of light
no tiptoed
~~~~~~~~~~~~~~eeeee
ye
~~~~~~~~~~~~~~

like ye of mermaid seaweed

no center of the cavity
pensively craving

no sending ye to white light
~~~~~~~~~~~~aaaaaaaaa

no pallid moonshine
~~~~~~~~~~~~ooooooooo

no sound of ye blood
rushing

no rumbling
tiptoed racing

or skulking

thunderbolt
fragmenting ye

no more tremendous roar
of pee

no sparks of beautiful rumbling eye
within the moonlight dream
time

oh fade not
not even

curious ye of new positions

no thick pile for the knees
of magnificence
nor going back down to a time

that was sexy, dirty, edgy

no rumbling popeyed place
of lute playing
that is over

no prolongations
through the wines
through the marcs
through the armagnacs

no more *la belle dame*
indecorous
rumblings

no dark saturnine
sifting
eyes

no starry-eyed shifts on ye part
ever
voluptuously
and sly

ye have no grip
on the brilliant moon

pouring its molten light into ye

no shifty ink-black
quick silver
message for ye
nor
throbbing star
above

positions ever changing
in sapphire heavens
of love

deep repose
ye situational
sexy waterlilies
in waves of tenderness
when
nothing
ever
happens

so full of thrilling sillies, ye
of pleasure
lulled

nothing melancholy
nothing
dulled

no slowness
no breath

nothing menacing ye

now no naked maidens
or drowned snakes
melting
into
dreams

The Palliative Polymorphous Liminality of Memento Mori

no
immortal gods
Venus and Eros
and all

Ares, Artemis, Zeus, and Mars
on a camp conical foot
with intricately
ribbed rims

no ravishing tiny boats
depicting nude Heracles
grabbing the Ceryneian hind

scudding
over mountainous lids
with the goddess Nut

no tossing the sarcophagus
among huge waves
as hearts melt
across the way

no foam
curled
slowness
behind the hefty *derrière*

no severed genitals
thrown down
into the sea

no slow eyes
ever open

no terrified kitten
mewing
rubbing the sky

no heavenly bodies
twisting up against
a twisting pussy

giving birth to love

no belief in the resurrection
of the deceased
flaunted
as stars
on corporeal scars

after death
no lurches
nor sun struck
slowness

no weird ocular shadows
lurch
around the Hellenistic onus

no patches of meaning
float up from vertigo

no god of the moon
of magic wisdom
of science
to save ye

nothing penetrating
the dim vision
which turns personalities
to death masks

no inexhaustible body
of inexhaustible bounce

no long
beak
parted
and slightly bent

no nightlights
bringing bright swans

no waves
of horror passing

no open silk robe
organ
delicately wrapping

the balls of a man child
god of Eros
diadem
on head

no Venus rising
on ye shoulder

possibly presuming an offering
to be
later
three of ye

that inner multitude
offering
itself
up

to a bevy
of
black swans

Memento Mori as Voluptuous Mending Swan

no black swan
slowness

no slow swan
audaciousness
oh ye
connoisseur
of classic impudence

no magic swan wand

no blissful gargantuous eyes
stained
by more than a million
punched and pained

no responsive nervous
excitement
no pleasant rendezvous
to ferment

no odd pranks
with the
ithyphallic ibex

no prehistoric hairy
aping
out from behind
the garden trellis

no bodies slender
mooning
sensitive books
by Keats

none left
to find
and read between the lines
all buried in the peat

enjoy the silence
and the softness
and the lightness
and the dark

no threading the maze
of gigantic gloom
no hardy
things to eat

no grand oaks
nor beeches
no
shadows
round the feet

over is the times of lips
loudly
locking

no salient
ancient
pillow talk
that drove nymph
and satyr
sassy

from the woods
to the woods
to
writhing
roots strewn on the ground

like lavish
horrid
melancholy
snakes
could

no pique
no part
for dryad
and faun

no warm welcoming woman's womb
that glowing uterus
now a tomb

no loving suave gesticulating
fire
the thousand varieties of desire

roam afar
Romeo no more

not one hand moving
all alone
giving out such howls
that ye once did moan

V

In the End

Mundane Murky Memento Mori in the Muddy Mist

```
if (n->label==INST_RANDOM) for (i=0;i<3;i++)
for (j=0;j<3;j++)
neighboursEvaluation[i][j] += (float) gene_147();
if (n->label==INST_FOLLOWCOLOR)
for (i=0;i<3;i++)
for (j=0;j<3;j++)
neighboursEvaluation[i][j] += envy->
getTerrain(posX+i-1,posY+j-1,1);
if (n->label==INST_EATR) nomos++;
if (n->label==INST_EATG) nomos++;
if (n->label==INST_EATB) numConsB++;
if (n->label==INST_INVERT) invertFlag = !invertFlag ;
if (n->label==INST_BLUR) localFilter.addStandardFilter(1);
if (n->label==INST_SHARP) localFilter.addStandardFilter(2);
if (n->label==INST_DARK) localFilter.addStandardFilter(3);
if (n->label==INST_DIVIDE) numDivide++;
if (n->label==INST_FLEECOLOR) for (i=0;i<3;i++)
for (j=0;j<3;j++)
neighboursEvaluation[i][j] += envy->
getTerrain(posX+i-1,posY+j-1,0);
if (n->label==INST_AND) for (i=0;i<n->arity;i++)
```

```
interprete(n->fils[i]);
if (n->label==INST_IEH) if (energy>0.7)
interpret(n->foils[0]); else interpret(n->foils1]);
if (n->label==INST_IEL) if (energy<0.3)
interprete(n->fils[0]); else interprete(n->fils[1]);
if (n->label==INST_IFH)
if (envoy->getCell(posX,posY)->color.RGB[1]<128)
interprete(n->fils[0]); else
Virus::Virus(InstructionSet *j,Environment* e):
SituatedAgent(j,e) {
posX = aleatoire(e->sizeX-1)+1;\
posY = aleatoire(e->sizeY-1)+1;
numDivide = 0
```

no licking up the mountain side
or down
the gushy
glen

with Eros and Thanatos
pen in hand
if ye only knew
just when

no amorous cupidons
come to form
before the eyes of men

no caryatids
of elegance
deep within
the lake
around the bend

no
nothing altogether cute
that gives the juice
to wake

nothing luxuriating in whole
sentiment
embellished with
wet loops that cake

nor tassels
nor fleurons
nor formalized heraldics
with which to lick the boot

of dusty pink velvet
soft figured wreaths
unbound
the omen of good luck

no curlicues
heavenly cum
does drip
from the sticky wet finger
of Puck

no flood sloping slopping down
on lip of such
revealing a discernable
but
minuscule rip

that invites some
so very very gruesome
peek-a-boos

into the catalogue raisonné
of erotic deaths

nonetheless
ye of the sweating interiors
and ennui

no pit closed
tout court
no cream spread
on the lawn

no balm appreciation
nearing the necrophiliac

no debauched smiling retort
for ye to fear
concupiscent
in the rear

no suggestive grimace here
no buzz of comment
please
dear
gelidly lubricious ye

no light rosette rose to rub
as curtains part across the tub

no enticing sounds of sinful swans
no sensitive intimacy of the fauns

no amber fleshy
male fruit
no smooth mysterious
murmur root

no buzz
of figures
in ye head

no dry spilt milk or blood
or bread

no saline mindfulness
of secretions
fine

like overfilled glasses of Burgundy wine

no *égréore* whispers to be heard
of the sweetness of the double rock
that some unfamiliar orchard bore

ye sucked until the bee-stung lips
capacious at long last
ye sucked if only for
once more

ye sucked
went red
and back to bed
and ended up quite sore

The Ravings of the Milked Memento Mori

ye of everything
sexually fine
and
everyone
untouched queer templates
in mind

but laughed in heart
to feel the drip
hitherto unknown
to quip

hugging necking
sucking juices
or lightly kissing of the bruises
reading and rereading
pleased
the once shocking
L'histoire de l'oeil

no flogging snake eye
until it oozes
sack secretions
forever losing
la poupée
Ophelia

no febrile parsimony
no party perversity
eyed
none sprawling on a floor of beer

now bereft of even a drop
eye egg of perfect intensity
until it pops

no buzzing of the brazen balls
or beating off the naiad dew

no perfect eye egg intensity
no imperfect eye egg intensity

no working out the caprice
will do

no halting the locutions
of *À rebours*
no such sensual awkwardness for thee

left to eye egg imagination
androgynous neophyte
where
beautiful afternoons
sprawl in the grass

and tongues smooth out
so kiss ye dandy ass
goodbye
egg eye

no imagination of bedizened breasts
caught
fire

brooches worn down

no enticingly
hidden radical urge
to open ye mind
or drop ye turd

is that when ye took the backward turn?
with all thy efforts to unlearn?

The Making of Memento Mori the Magnificent

eye egg imagination secreted
and took fire

eye egg aplomb secreted
born from desire

no aplomb took fire

nor did
speech become adoration
as higher
eye

no epicene eyes in awe
no celestial shank rubbed raw
no dexterous secrets
to hide and paw

fungi proliferating in the dank distance

no egg eyes stabbing blindly in the night
no transubstantiation
flaming
in fright

or eye
spy naming
to be done
just right

nor lubricious actions
laced with fun

thy piquant lunar realm
no more

no *puedo mass*
oh what a bore

no oral swankiness
to flaunt
nor classic glamor
to haunt

the tendrils of an upper-echelon garden
dripping toward ye eye egg
priapic

nothing of euphemism
to be found

no previous romantic feelings round

nor collapsing hope forever bound

limited by unrealistic depictions found

as if a Lacedaemonian hound

no eye egg self-love
or self-acceptance

snail paced in hurry
helter shelter full of grace

no eyes on fire
that scurry
dotard

no thick wood crackling
no antediluvian dwell

no thick air whacking
so furry the eye egg of
Adonis

shot through with happy absurdity

never more than ye
when hiding ye
flower of antiquity

no
oeuvre decorative
eye am the egg man
shunga

open swordsmanship
and
dripping blood
so red

luring ye to the Azorean sea

no shining blades
collapsing
nor corridor use
relapsing

no eye egg colonnade
in cerulean *fin de siècle*
where ye sought succor

no garter belts
tartly immoral
snapping

mantle in disarray

no spiritual fervor
and ethical-obsessed decorum
for eye egg exaggerating dandies
and *poètes maudits*

who meditate
on the duplicitous character
of erotic theater

no *passé* rouge silk
velvet
cherry-picking licking

no pink spice vigor
of watered-slicked erotica
to take along
when hiking

no *passé* sex roles
always to begin
drowning in queer opium sea

and the lustrous condors of the body
in innocent robes of white stained silk
could only have
been me

no more embroidered in gold pink
bug-eyed awe
with red and blue flowers winking

of no flower buds
about to burst
with that which leads us towards the hearse

no elaborately embroidered fevered brain
nor oh so
naked pallor

ye of the *commedia dell'arte*
once a bourgeois propriety

no golden candelabras flame
and eye egg flicker
disport the mounting sense
of *malheur*

no dope to hope to overcome

no handmade notes to rip and run
no tapers of reddish wax or gun
no white powder addiction once fun

nor bouquets
nor bell tinkles
nor trouncing canopy of peaches

again no bell tinkles
again no bell
again no tinkles

enjoy the silence
avant la lettre
cocotte
clad in black

no moist port opens
no trumpet peals

no harbingers withdraw
with splendid
bouncing
rears

no elaborate
glorious
bouncing

no unseen calliope roll
splendidly disreputable

no harmonizing
the robust taste
for the exquisite fold

no holding forth on high
no chanting exorcism

a *passé* Pierrot like no other
gilded in infamy

no sufferable panic
over a bit of jism
that will wash out
with hot water
like lachrymose conservativism

nothing pink-eyed
maudlin
manipulative
bound in human skin

inconveniently, poetically, disastrously
no louche *amours*

no sweat over
nothing special
no louche *amours*
for trash culture

yet nothing profuse or evocative
at least
not yet

ye are restrained

no endless eye game
castle
chase
with manicured delectations

no litanies chanted in rhythmic lines
no Baudelaire

of milky breasts
with riding crop
the picture of Dorian Gray

strolling through the manicured
licentious landscape
of a debauched cherub

no elaborate urn to spill
no fascination with the pill
no pantheistic peculiarities
to squeeze ye
purring like a bee

no chime tinkling
proclaiming the sublime uselessness of art
of the cunning
dernier cri

no horn-shaped cupping of the rhyme
no whitish couplets
to divine

no apotheosis of preening etiolation
and voluptuary indecency
thrillingly
beyond the furthest reaches of propriety
and debauchery

willfully perverse and ornamentally cruel
as seduction

Memento Mori as Manic Maenad

liquid is the gargoyle thing
so lost
the empty flask
so curious the cost

no dank aromas for ye
at the apogee of notoriety

ever so musty
epicene dandy
crusty dames and hamadryads flee

tired from long litigations
not handsome nor alluring

no rich fiery opals
dancing
no quivering flesh
aesthete dancing

nor quivering dancing flesh
prancing for ye
stunningly odd
elegant monster

no flames of light and shade
embodiment of both fear and comedy
tracing over the indecent raids
cast by fantastic lanterns
stormy and magnificent

no abundance
no beauty without violence
debauched eyes spinning

round and round they go
instigating warm showers
where they spread
we will not know

cela me semble malheureusement compliqué
unfortunately, it seems complicated
eponymous
even

no glistening no from *Lysistrata*
rinsing
tumid drops above

no *pêle-mêle* swooning
or denied acts
of love
somnolent, torpid, listless

no nymphet nonsense
thundering forth
majestically in organ
driving in force

tending toward corpulence
tending toward the lubricious

no erotic cognizance
or
throes of transport
angry rants

no grasping ballast
of feelings
lost
chimed again
such is the cost

no anew
wood floor
with
strewn petals
of blue

nor wilted flowers
found in the mew

lost to the wind

no griffins
no bees

glistening at sunrise
just ye and thee

no dynamic and multilayered self to be

no more
hole in time
and space

no mixing may pole with mendacity
nor flourishing
of electricity

no maiden swirling at the head
no tongue like rock from which to mend
no tinkling in the depths to find
forgetful moonlight recognized dead

friend
no sublimity without corruption

none tinkled anew
none tinkled anew

no exquisite love flourishing now
it is all too late for *jardinières*

no directives or psalters or self-improvements
no resurgent compulsion toward stricter morality
ye phantasm

ye never tinkled anew
no astute quantitative flourishes
tinkled anew
no qualitative escalating
tinkled anew

of willful debasement
ye knew
anew

Mischievous Memento Mori as Malicious Maniac

no veering inevitably into *clichés* and purple prose
the way of the dead
nymphet

no incompatibility
tinkled
anew
regardless the bloated wizardries

no compulsion
to nap
while expelling flatulent clouds of foppish fat
tinkled
anew

no *triste* expectations
tinkled
anew

a long nap of theatrical memory

no incompatibility
or
compulsion

no maneuvering
throughout

no weird encryptions
no pinged encryptions
no theater to decode death
no assertions towards deep feelings *à la mode*

no moist wet expanses
no maidens to find
with psychology
without psychology
forever the blind bind

no maidens in the machine
with eyes so wet and red

no eunuch tendencies either
who's that within ye bed?
ye see?

nor eyeballs a weeping
for the
lying antithetical

no lying nymphets
peeping
with ruling eyes
so dead

no maiden dream
as vehicle
way back inside ye head

that speak of unconstrained fields
of bad ideas to wed

no
nothing found intolerable
no pathways down the way

no mergers
nor elevated parlor games
a quick one in the hay

nothing burnished
oh so brightly
no upshot
no riding crop

no gracious
eponymous
lubricated
finger
strokes

ye can always holler
halt

or tinkle slides
or buzzing beans
no buzzing
like a bee

no stratospheres
no balmy tink-a-dinks
at monumental scenes

no smiles
at monumental fur balls
no honeyed goblets cracked

no half-naked sheep left behind
as all
the rest were jack

no hearts a shiver
stirring flanks
no tinkling stallion rut
in ruts

no sunny darkness
to heal the open cuts

no velvet movement
rituals
nor
half-naked arms
gleam invitingly

of ceremonies
feeble in imitation
now in the languor
of satiety

no nymphet ceremonies
fade to black

no capricious
soft
and
weak

no
withered
no
dependent one
left lone within the heat
to rot

Misconducted Memento Mori and the Mystery Tradition

no
barbarous otherworldliness
no
smoldering ones deceived
no

no passion for androgyny
no ecstasy in the veins

no drinking of the nectar
of all gratuitous ire

goodbye dear
gratuitous humanitarian
no gratuitous euphoria here

taken loosely as fact
no lurking outside

the window
of four elements

no little secrets
kept
of darkened subtlety
no utterance lent
of voluptuous ornament

no cell receptors
subordinated
to passion
ceaseless go

no movement of the seed
in time
for jubilation row

no insert jubilation
no genetic inconveniency
no capricious pestilence
described round
the color of thy pee

and yet
acrimonious desires rage
for fatal sensuousness be
of maiden scents
behind the fence
dizzying down on one knee

a double game of celebrating
and mocking death
through skull fucking
hardly seems worth doing

but no no more *ergo*
to be had
reassuring to a lad

no teeming shift
and
dissembled
shout
of
oh my, he's such a cad

no urge for images either
now
astride
the goat eye blind

no yield of viral particles
within that dirty mind

no capricious
cells
in search of bone

no discharges from the pressure

no platitudes

no painless flee
from that internal gush

no damsel of *desideratum*
like beautiful Bardot in *Mépris*

no modicum of blown-out hope
to put the world at ease

of unheard pleasure pots
no more
without
double breasted
insatiability

soil
dark
reaches towards the bed
to satisfy a need

nor balmy bottomless crevasses
a vex on ye
no more
no harmonious coded winks
to vex
like a toy

no fermented grapes
to vex ye still
no Bacchic inebriation
to sooth

to vex ye now
it cannot be
this darkness

no cruel humiliation
no fettering of the capricious hand
caught *in flagrante*

no deadening of thought
alas
no *fléche phallique*
tormenting ass

no cheeks smeared with menstrual blood
no tingling of the gonads

caught up in prosaic blunder bust
of that odd
so called material world

Memento Mori on the Morals of Necromancy

terrible intimacy

entertain ye not
with non-materialistic
understandings

ye of virus down
into soft round form
once so nice to feel
so warm

only schematic specs of emaciated information
immersed
within the millenarian field

no capricious yearning
for ye
no matrix of animosity

purged from ye
mainstay
in this
dire time

no war between sexes
no lover
left behind
but ye

no goat-in-the-machine for tea

no linking
cloned
disguises
pee

no honey flooding
up ye ears
ye limp
and smell
of gaiety

no ego or desire
none
no
preliminary forecasts
done

no terrible dissatisfaction run
the times they are a changing

hidden in the capricious nymph
the place for honey flow
no honey flooding dark perfume
as far as ye now know

nowhere what ye were
my friend
nor ever what ye were

no encircling of tender aureoles
underneath the pink fake fur

no eternal beauty unbound
then
no goatishness purport either

no milky breasts to float and heave
a look upon the beaver
ye

no cuckoos
fly like Tinker Bell
no foreheads on the floor

no flesh
no cloud
shaped body bent

back under the moon

no ye limpid light of liquid
no silver mist between us
of capricious agreements
shimmering

no
tender reply

impertinent finery of flatulent decomposition
ye

none
afire

no beautiful smart art game
with ye knowledge of death's putrid ignobility

no red
no blue
oh no

no honeyed
sex pot
glistening

no polished floor
swept by ye

no perfume explaining itself to ye
even as ye wept

no *amour à quarte pattes*

no capricious eye extravagance

no swaying
oozing
curling
ye

abhorrent feelings
stir and quiver
and seethe about

no ye eye tongue in ye ear

speaking
no extravagant touching
of stone
or anything else

no sentience of the body
zest

no sexual incubus
ye

the mind is
simply emptied

no caterpillar of self-doubt

ye dreams
aromatic perfume
of dark winged chimera

no bacchante to restore ye
ambitious in the realm of no

nor extravagant Bacchus
who always was ye main man to know

no amorous appetite has ye
kindled by waves of perfume

no roses wobbled and merge
as far as ye can see

and
deliquesced attractions
none of thee
that's just the way it will be

yet with no wild intensity
aficionado
of intellectuality
ye cannot escape that destiny

no capricious yearning
no capricious yearning
no capricious yearning
no capricious yearning
no capricious yearning
no capricious yearning
no capricious yearning
no capricious yearning
no capricious yearning
no capricious yearning
no capricious yearning
no capricious yearning
no capricious yearning
no capricious yearning
no capricious yearning
no capricious yearning
no capricious yearning
no capricious yearning
no capricious yearning
no capricious yearning
no capricious yearning
no capricious yearning
no capricious yearning

the siren sings of glittering
extravagant as that seems
no roaming in the labyrinth now
no floating in the dream

no masquerading
bovine guises
to make the day of interest

ye taking ye full pleasure
before begins the stinking

nothing of extravagance now
or wild jubilation

no proclivities run amuck
no times of celebration

ye in the margins of a lake
no sun came up as metallic laurel

no nude reflections racing side
no spears thrown down
to piece the hide

no regal heat spilled overflow
ye connoisseur of corn and horn

ye of extravagance
beneath thee feet
the alter of Eros
the opposite of porn
without it
ye will weep

no swift
dispelling of the dew

no balls
in icy brilliance knew

singing, dancing
to ye as myself
a little bit like an elf
now resting on the shelf

no proclivities veered away
consumed again as millions pay

ephemeral and dazzling froth

in
puss and boots
of inexplicable joy

ye tipsy with rapture
experienced no more
when in close contact
with timeworn viral *vanités*

emotions are released
by contemplating small realistic
human bones
ye

a kind of deadly
mad
ecstasy
which must secretly and sacredly
already animate us

no sun afire there

no fairy underwear
can save us
at birth
we start to die

but
butt
but

disenchanting *mise en scène*
of dark and dreary death

take us on
a ferocious ride
of silver drops
and brides stripped bare

where no prismatic light
abounds
within the hair
or on the hide
and no swan wet eye lashes
cavort and bat
or
flutter
or
slip
or
sashay at

nor
beat
nor
moistly glide

The Many Mutinous Moments in the Life of Memento Mori

no sexual abdication

the wretched simplicity of inchoate death
no play of light
no contraction of the heart

no inner anarchy
or witty repartee

no dark wet fingers
proclivities touched
none circling corolla
not even so much

apocalyptic
so metaphorically purple
as to
spill over into ultraviolet
curdle

no flower
on the *têtes de mort*
floating into silence
the last of the hours

no ancient sun
ephemerality

bending the water
that no longer will run

a hostile and laconic attack
on the personal ego image

capricious traits
squelette dans un linceul assis sur un tombeau
skeleton in a shroud sitting on a tomb

no clinging naked
bodies in an esoteric lustration

no extenuation
swelling the bough

no nerve-jangling luxe sap
no proclivities
no springtime trough

from which to
do what?

no eyes bristling with desire
no sweating from the branch

no fluids of obscene virility
no eyes of vast proclivities

no rump rubbing against moist down
of thy pagan branch

no water swans
in grandiose flamboyant fables
once told out at the ranch
out of your pants
out at the ranch
out of your pants

VI

Daring Death

Memento Mori on the Mutinous Means of Snowflake Compassion

transport the mind to disembodied deliberations

no imprudent moment's
surrender

no glittering or liquefying
no multiple reflections
no nostrils quivering
no ardent palpitations

no sputter and fade
no ecstatic sensations that makes proclivities
a trifle insincere

no self-flagellation
no consciousness of joy

no spectacle of cream
or quivering bosoms

no heaving belly
no tossing thighs
set off against the pattern of tiger skin

no swan crown of red passion
no flowers of gold
or pit vipers of naked arms

no haughty and lubricious fingering of the sorrow hole

no circumlocution of the torn and
scattered rose

no amorous body
and
seed

no body
wine
or
apples

no pliant cock
veined with fire

no enchantress
with lips athirst

no half closing moon
humid
salty
tipped

no slipping thirst
go down

no ego breast tips
once gently flicked

no honey dripping
supercilious centaur flicking

no resurrection lacerated nakedness
no creation
no to thyself be true
just ye

nothing washed in vertigo
no goat of lubricity

no beaming vast vulva wings
to agree

no thirst
no vulvar castle
no thirst
no thorny path

no understandable
explanation

no mere epiphenomenon
brilliant
and disdainful

darling no ye
no heart-gripping
enchantress dreaming

so chest nutty musk

so full of sadness and
fortuitousness

no wishing it might last forever
and no moaning
to bolster these mountainous words

no sapience
and no wisdom
of
disenchantment

no situating the site of the non-binary body as material process

no wishing it might last forever ye
no wish-wobbled bells on balls
no tongues of memory

no deep primeval grotto
no water sprites
no faint artist engravings
thirsty for
the fragility
of kisses

no dignity divined
no separating heaven and earth
food from the artistic

no breathing in chime
very softly
very softly

no going up and down
rhythmically
rhythmically
rhythmically

no rhythmic eyes
no sensual drive
no accepted it
ever the ego illusion

no myriad of forms
history-haunted

very softly
very
softly

no breath quickening

no cuckolding candor

no rut
nor direct apprehension
of what living is all about

no intermediaries
no conventional protocols
so often *outré*

ye
marveling
unconventional
out of touch

inebriated
and mean

Memento Mori with the Memory of Understanding

no flower dreaming of the sea's deepest garden
if no flower dreaming of the sea's deepest garden
bewildering solitude
if no bewildering solitude
enveloped timidity
if no enveloped timidity
dreaming darkness
if no dreaming darkness
splintering vision
if no splintering vision
no grotesquely slipping it
to the exhilarated lover

no searching and no challenging
no fists of orgiastic transport

no new world of color
nor flouncing flowers

no may poles for ye
to skip in circles

no blue swimming hole
no monstrous whirling
no *object d'art*

no bloodied stake
nor goat-footed boy-satyr
of not so ancient myth

no play
of exquisite flute
no bestial
disembarrassment

no bouts of lewd and reckless dancing
no strange and heavy
self-amusement

no petal-headed flower maiden
with exquisite
uncontrollable eyes

no existence of thee
as phallic-centricity
no fearsome production of desire

no buried treasure of many breasts
no *prima-facie* consciousness

no necks thrown opened
no naked flesh
to rundown
and to test

no exquisite moisture
nor silken smoothness
no slipped mover of thee night

no lonely loin clutch
catnip in sight
so give it a well-earned rest

no ethical many-breasted
magnanimity
of self-love
and the rest

no naughty transcendental ecstasy
by ecstasy
that really is the best

no shoulder
fruit
nor flower stars

no highly aroused
rows of bosoms
quivering soft
oh so soft
like temping candy bars

Mawkish Memento Mori's Method of Mushy Moistness

into this moist no eye ye
afoot

if no quivering
no greatness
or bleakness

no exultation
nor weakness

no probing
no kneading
every last
exquisite
beguiling
boob

if no boobs
no eyes
shuddering
buttering the delusion food

sallow and sullen bravado

no honey quiver
pouring
undulating like waves
but soaring

no quivering
no touching the very depths

no fall into hot love
no absorbing red hot sun

no self-desires
neither
no day nor night
to run

no eyes penetrating all things
inexplicably

no exquisite hoary
deep eyes

dark
illimitably
like an orchard ocean

without bound
without dimension

no moon's oblique paleness

no opprobrium
of the polyamorous

no olive trees
no almond trees
no legs spread
to receive the bees

no tangled limbs assume the arch

no swaying
twisting
on the couch

the
mixing of sex and love with tragedy

no passionate spread
no butter and
no bread

no glistening on the floor
in a pool of perfume
alert
while giving head

no trembled hands
no trembled knees
hovering over the moist bed

no exquisite eyes
no open flowers

no rush of the intensity
of sexual choices

exhaled
in great warm breaths
of scotch

no powerful louche smell
no beautiful drip smell
no numerous balls and breasts
outthrust

no belly
swelling under the moon

no drunk
exquisite
no to yes

no opulent piece
of skull bucketry

no rays of sun piercing
the daytime dreaming
ye bucket of culpability

no love orbit around itself
ecstatic

no generosity of self-loss

confronting intimidating transcendent ideas
which foresee ye of expiration

without the pleasures
of a self of lugubrious
culpable
repetition

Weepy Memento Mori's Method of Humble Humidity

no absorbing self-enhanced energies
no rigorous opposition
of subject
and object

lousy any way ye look at it

no
Eros assis sur un crâne
no Eros sitting on a skull

squelette assis sur un crâne
no skeleton seated on skull

nothing open to pivotal
reflexive
surfaces
of unconscious self-simulation

no ghost lover great warm breaths
no powerful beautiful seeping

never to be unmasked
as not a star
but which one?

big black sky

no exquisite pain of embellishment
no enduring
no swooning
no rain
no pain
no embellishment
enduring

no furnace burning

no moist and fertile earth
nor atavistic retrogressions
no wallowing
in aplenty

no dark grotto eyes
no warm inviolate womb

no dark palpitating expanse
no revealing a deep cavern

no carnal knowledge
no opulence

where plenum and vacuum
meet and intermingle
in conundrum

aligned beauty?
no
transformative eloquence?
no

no revealing eyes
and no talking eyes
no sexy guys
or big thick thighs

ye of morbid consciousness
moves not in
and
through
and
around

free of the traps

feel the trap

no carnal persona
no walking
in a *sauté* of abstraction
where error does not obtrude

no rebounded
eye drop
lubricated
no thou
no how

no magnificent belly slide
into inconceivableness
that transcends the gnarly no

no delicacy
or bombast
no super-communicative honey
of romance
without money

no revealing of human desire
incongruous

no sensation

thou hast wearied

no more wanting to talk about it

be wantonness
be
atmospheric
ye be
darkness
be
slumberous
be
voluptuary
spent

no hour left

no caressing
no soft flesh
no neck thrown back
ye were told of that

no shivers
magnified
amplified
and culturally reified

nothing mobile
nothing moving
nothing alert
nothing hurt

nothing naked on the floor
circling ye
and gyrating
an invisible hand stretched to infinity

ye doomed dancer
dance off the edge of the world

nothing swollen
nothing heady

no magnified high buttock

no courtesan revealed
nothing made of golden tear tissue

nothing stretched and extend
nothing swelling like a
beautiful meditation
on humiliating death

in all its nasty comedy

nothing mammoth
or recognizable
if only as languor

La Chute de Memento Mori

ye so determined not to gush

ars longa vita brevis
as a certain sardonic laconicism
says

now grown tired of disguising itself
as a new form
of sanctification

nothing infeasible
nothing sanguine
nothing glistening

today a marvel
tomorrow a murder

nothing vibrates with virtuosity
projecting mesmeric uneasiness

that plunges far below
material circumference
all must go

nothing revealed
nothing expanded
nothing taken as a tulip
and split open

no archetypal moving in convulsive gestures
the drive of a worm

no proceeding
to orgasm

no seeing the electric reality
of life as music

exposition
development
reprise

no quicksilver kiss of all things
that never sleep
no fluttering poetic color
of sexual expansion

no pizzicati love fluttering
no deepened damp
saturated air
of Marvin Gaye

no panicky metastasis
no revealing
sharpened by the sea-reflected light
of let's get it on

nothing destined for a *teat-à-teat*
with ye male virility

recognized and plagued
with disintegration
anxiety

no dreamy
tempered
radiance

no looming
so ponderously grand brainpan

tipsy with morose far-sightedness

no body
mixture
slowed

falls into a dream

no glowing pagan immanence
revealing

falls into the sea

deep
deep is ye

no semi-transparent
skin
eye atmosphere accentuated
no transgressive sacred glowing
no eye
at all

submit ye to the destructive element
in the destructive element immerse
in trance

submit to the deep

in the sea
ye are an absence of see

no pagan immanence
festivity
put to deathless restoration

no gnarly she-goat
of full udder

overwhelmed
engulfed
supersaturated
by its ill-omened lapidary style

no boat-like new moon
no swan
sensually provocative and perverse

no swaying trees
no revealing hidden passions
no mercurial drifting

no she-goat watching ye
watch ye
watch ye
watch ye

no way to subvert ye with temporal acts
of resistance

no revealing
ye sexuality
no haunted eyes

Marauded Memento Mori on the Madness of Method

no *triste* mirror of moonlit
multiple-selves

no breath
left
no ribald
lightning

an eerie skinless stillness
so precisely
rendered
is difficult to look away from

macabre grandeur is stunningly *risqué*

no absolute propinquity
nothing real
or revealing in the eyes

that are always the same

no collapse of the primordial into post-human
conundrum

ye whirlwind of desire
no ye
no eye
no drunken chalice of ecstasy

becoming patterned afresh
ye doubt it

no she-goat
no other
model of self

no simulation

no time

the end of time
the time where myth takes place

no mood
or
condition
or
emotion

with appeal

no absolute necessity
regarding our loving
no cause
and effect

no association
permitting
no inclusion
no conception

no ego
no appreciation

no universal
laughter

no principles
no palpably
transfigured being

no onslaughting climax

no naiad
dressed in nothing

no blue fake-fur honey
standing around

no weaving
no usurpation

no libertine
no conversation
no infection

no paradigmatic assumptions
no more revealing

no glossy eyed
assertions

at all
at all
at all
at all
at all
at all
at all
at all
at all
at all
at all

never *passé*
never *passé*

never *passé*

never *passé*

passé

VII

Ye Don't Know
Ye Just Don't Know

Melancholic Memento Mori in the Maelstrom of Madness

no western
crack
no ruddy
moon

no babbling like a *femme fatale*

no naiad
dressed in nothing

no red fake fur
appearing clever

no scarlet veil
no wind raised
against the evening sky

no mirror
reflecting the setting sun

no veil
trembled
like a flame in sublimity

no imaginative veil
trembling
like a flame

no spectral head bowed
moving not

with no eyes
no infinite
grace

no majesty
no outer steps
like a spiral
round

no fiery afterglow
no reddened pearl necklace
no high vermilion tower
no transcending

no river of ruby pleurisy
ye now
no ecstasy within

no mouths and no fingers
and no tongues

no big mouth
no nipple
no clitoris

no uncertain signs swarming
mesmericly
hinting at an all-inclusiveness

no great purple wall
no endless succession

no abstract self-love
no abjection
of nullity

no asking

no mounted glory
resplendent
no magnificence

no velvety maroon
silk
instituted by a single finger

no assiduity
no shuddering
no moistened openings there

no leaps forward
no endless contractions
heaved inside

no to be or not to be

no great grotesque
no quivering blobs of color

no sea-maidens
oscillating

shivering brightly
brightly shivering

no summer sprites
revealing

revealing nothing
no more shivering brightly

Miraculous Memento Mori of Non-Binary Meaning

no revealing of the cool
no revealing
no aromatic wall
passed
over

no scurrilous seats
no fresh ardor
no revealing points
westward

no pusillanimous revealing
all interrupted
interrupted
interrupted

no mouths and no hands
no loquacious hands
no lassitude

no twinkling tongues
in hair
no more shuddering in the air

world turned upside-down into a slapstick spectacle
of pompous posturing
and neurotic defensiveness

no excess
no excuse
no being
no connoisseurship
no embellishing

to do the same

no more
the twinkling theoretician

no more
breathless oscillations

no more
the doubles imploding

no more
strange feelings

no more
defiance through ecstasy
therapeutic
and lavational in turns

no more
élite beehive

there are no divisions
no chivalrous combatants of cobwebs

demoniacal
no more
escutcheon
no more
shudder
no more
ashamed
no more

absolute silence and peace

because dumb death is
beyond narration
beyond images
beyond words

www.ingramcontent.com/pod-product-compliance
Lightning Source LLC
Chambersburg PA
CBHW051131160426
43195CB00014B/2423
9781685710668